Original title:
Aerial Pegs Beyond the Griffin Hemp

Author: Liina Liblikas
ISBN HARDBACK: 978-1-80563-451-5
ISBN PAPERBACK: 978-1-80564-972-4

Chasing Shadows Above the World

In twilight's veil, the shadows dance,
With whispered tales of fate and chance.
They weave through trees, a fleeting song,
A passage where the brave belong.

Each step we take, they seem to sway,
In search of peace, we lose our way.
Yet in the dusk, a spark ignites,
To guide us forth through endless nights.

With every breath, the whispers grow,
A promise wrapped in moonlit glow.
In shadow's arms, we find our role,
A quest that binds the heart and soul.

Statues of Cloud and Dream

Upon the hill where dreams take flight,
Stand statues wrought of cloud and light.
Their forms, a dance of soft embrace,
In every curve, a timeless grace.

Whispers of hope in quiet tones,
They cradle dreams like precious stones.
Beneath the sky's enchanting hue,
These sentinels keep watch for you.

When storms arise, their strength holds fast,
In storms and shadows, they will last.
A tethered bond between the two,
Where earth meets sky in shades of blue.

Symphony of the Feathered Realm

In branches high, the songbirds trill,
A symphony that bends the will.
With every chirp, a note of cheer,
Their melodies, the heart can steer.

They dance on air, in vibrant hues,
In sunlit skies or morning dews.
Each beat a promise, bright and clear,
A glimpse of joy that draws us near.

Through forests deep where shadows creep,
Their songs awaken dreams from sleep.
Each feathered warble, wise and free,
Unfolds the wonders yet to be.

The Sky's Embrace of Mystery

Beneath the veil of starry night,
The sky unfolds its hidden light.
A tapestry of tales untold,
In cosmic whispers, secrets unfold.

Through shifting clouds, the moonlight beams,
A sanctuary for wandering dreams.
With every glance, we seek to know,
The mysteries where stardust flows.

As shadows brush the earth below,
The realms of magic start to glow.
In sky's embrace, our spirits soar,
In wonder, lost forevermore.

Harbingers of the Feathered Night

In shadows deep, the owls take flight,
With whispers soft, they greet the night.
Their wings embrace the velvet air,
A haunting call, both wild and rare.

They soar above the ancient trees,
With eyes like moons, they watch the breeze.
In silver light, the secrets weave,
Of stories lost, of those who grieve.

The stars align, a guiding spark,
As darkness spills, they leave their mark.
A tale unfolds in quiet grace,
Of feathered dreams in endless space.

When shadows dance upon the ground,
In every rustle, magic's found.
The night unfolds, a tapestry,
Where harbingers of dusk roam free.

When Myth Takes to the Skies

Above the realm where legends dwell,
The phoenix sings its fiery spell.
With vibrant plumage, bright and bold,
A story of rebirth is told.

The griffin glides on whispering gales,
With strength and grace, it never pales.
In hues of gold, it guards the night,
A sentinel of dreams in flight.

The dragon's roar, a mighty sound,
As stars align, its heart is bound.
To skies where wishes softly gleam,
In myth's embrace, we dare to dream.

When night descends, let spirits soar,
As ancient tales unlock the door.
With every wingbeat, stories rise,
In wonder woven through the skies.

Clouds of Whimsy and Reverie

In fields of blue, the dreams are spun,
With gentle hues of golden sun.
The clouds begin their playful dance,
In every shape, they weave romance.

A castle forms, a dragon flies,
In cotton skies, where laughter lies.
With every breeze, they shift and sway,
A world where magic finds its way.

The children gaze with wide-green eyes,
As whispers float from clouds to skies.
Each puff a tale, each shade a clue,
In realms of whimsy, fresh and new.

As dusk approaches, colors blend,
In twilight's embrace, the day will end.
Yet dreams alight on softest fluff,
In clouds of reverie, we feel enough.

The Dance of the Gilded Silks

In gardens lush where twilight blooms,
The silks of night dispel the glooms.
With every thread, a tale enchants,
As shadows swirl in twilight's dance.

The moonlight shimmers on the grass,
Where fireflies twirl and breezes pass.
Each fluttered wing, a soft embrace,
The beauty held in time and space.

With gilded hues, the stars ignite,
To twinkle dreams through velvet night.
Each whispered hope, a secret spun,
In silken threads, we all are one.

The dance unfolds, a timeless rhyme,
Where moments weave through space and time.
In every heart, a song ignites,
The magic lives in gilded nights.

The Horizon's Kiss of Enchantment

Across the hills where shadows play,
A whisper floats on twilight's breath,
The sun dips low, a golden ray,
Embracing night, it dances with death.

Stars awaken, shy and bright,
They pierce the velvet of the dark,
Enchanting dreams take flight tonight,
As hope ignites a tiny spark.

Moonbeams weave their silver strand,
Through branches swaying, soft and slow,
They guide the heart with gentle hand,
To places where the lost winds blow.

In the stillness, stories twine,
Of ancient realms and voices lost,
A tapestry of light divine,
Where every soul must pay the cost.

Each breath, a wish upon the breeze,
Each heartbeat, longing to transcend,
In twilight's grasp, we find our peace,
As night unfolds, the day must end.

Flights of Fancy and Folklore

In the meadow, secrets lie,
Where fairies flit 'neath daisies' glow,
Their laughter whispers to the sky,
Each tale a breeze that starts to flow.

Through the woods where shadows creep,
The stories weave in tangled threads,
Of daring dreams and wishes deep,
Awakening the hearts of fleds.

Eyes agleam with starlit schemes,
The moonlight casts a spell so bright,
While night becomes a canvas for dreams,
Where freedom soars, ousting the fright.

Each legend born from timeless lore,
Awaits the ear that dares to hear,
With wings unfurled, it starts to soar,
As dawn approaches, drawing near.

So let your heart ignite the night,
And chase the fables through the sky,
For in those tales, our spirits light,
Forever bound, we learn to fly.

Beneath the Gossamer Canopy

Underneath the ancient trees,
A world awaits in soft embrace,
Where whispers ride on gentle breeze,
And nature holds its sacred space.

Among the roots, the fairies dwell,
Crafting stars from whispered dreams,
In every leaf, a tale to tell,
In hidden glades, their magic gleams.

The twilight sighs, the shadows dance,
As fireflies flicker, winking bright,
Inviting all to take a chance,
To wander far through mystic night.

With every step, the heart can feel,
The magic stirring in the air,
An enchanting pause, a world surreal,
Where every glance unveils a prayer.

So linger here beneath the boughs,
Let gossamer wrap you in delight,
For in this realm, each heart avows,
That dreams take flight in endless night.

The Dance of Shadows and Skyline

In twilight's embrace, shadows take flight,
They twirl and they spin, a magical sight.
Whispers of secrets in the dim glow,
As night's gentle fabric begins to unfold.

Beneath the bright stars, a dance so divine,
A tapestry woven of dusk and moonshine.
Murmurs of laughter ride the cool breeze,
As dreams come alive in a world that can tease.

The city below, aglow in delight,
Looks up at the dancers, a feast for the night.
In silence they glide, on cobblestone paths,
Their movements are echoes of long-lost laughs.

With shadows entwined, they paint the night skies,
Crafting illusions that sparkle in eyes.
A moment suspended, in time it will stay,
As dawn gently whispers, farewell to the play.

Fables Suspended in the Air

Above the soft murmurs of passing dreams,
Fables take flight on delicate beams.
Stories of wonder on gossamer threads,
Whispered by winds to the hearts that are led.

A child's imagination, like feathers so light,
Holds worlds made of magic, a pure delight.
Each tale unfolds with a shimmer and glow,
Spanning the sky in a radiant show.

From dragons to wizards, adventures abound,
In realms where the brave and the kind are unbound.
Suspended in air, these fables take form,
Guiding the lost through the calm and the storm.

The laughter of stars joins the breath of the night,
As stories take shape in the silvery light.
Listen closely, dear hearts, as they venture and soar,
In the kingdom of dreams, there are always more.

Mysteries of the Ethereal Thread

Threads of the cosmos weave tales to behold,
In patterns of magic, their stories unfold.
Woven with starlight, they shimmer and sway,
Embracing the night in a luminous display.

Whispers of time cross this fabric of fate,
Beneath silver skies, where destinies wait.
Ethereal threads link the heart to the dawn,
Binding us gently, though shadows are drawn.

In glimpses of wonder, the unseen draws near,
Life's mysteries murmur, inviting our cheer.
Each strand a connection, a bond soft as air,
Promising secrets, if only we dare.

As we trace the patterns, our spirits will rise,
In the dance of the cosmos, let dreams be our guides.
For woven together, we're never alone,
In the tapestry of life, love always has grown.

Chronicles of the Skyward Connection

Upon the horizon, where earth meets the sky,
Chronicles whisper, like soft lullabies.
Beneath wings of starlings, the stories take flight,
Uniting our hearts in the canvas of night.

With hope in our souls, we reach for the gleam,
Tracing the paths of our collective dream.
Each twinkling star is a tale yet untold,
A beacon of courage for the timid and bold.

In the vastness above, we find our own place,
A constellation painted with love's warm embrace.
Skyward we look, as the universe calls,
Connected through time as its wonder enthralls.

So let us remember, as we gaze up so high,
The chronicles written in the depths of the sky.
With hearts intertwined, we are never apart,
In this boundless connection, we share every heart.

Whispers in the Sky

In twilight's embrace, the stars awake,
Silent stories, the night winds make.
Soft echoes weave through the darkened night,
Awakening dreams, taking flight.

Moonbeams dance on the silver streams,
Illuminating paths where the starlight beams.
Secrets linger in the cool night air,
Whispers of magic, beyond compare.

A tapestry spun from the heavens high,
Unraveled wonders, under the sky.
Glimmers of hope in the shadowed glade,
Where dreams are born and fears will fade.

Celestial Threads Unfurled

Beneath the heavens, we journey far,
Tracing the paths of each wandering star.
With every wish, a thread is drawn,
A tapestry woven, from dusk till dawn.

Celestial whispers through the night gleam,
Lifting our hearts in a shimmering dream.
The cosmos hums with a gentle tune,
As planets waltz beneath the moon.

With every heartbeat, the stardust flows,
In endless circles, the universe knows.
A dance of fate in the vast expanse,
Inviting us all to join in the dance.

The Flight of the Spun Dream

In the realm of dreams, where shadows play,
We drift on gossamer, light as the day.
A flight of fancy, so sweet and rare,
Carried on whispers, like soft summer air.

Each turn of thought spins a silken thread,
Weaving the wishes that dance in our head.
Up to the heavens our visions ascend,
A boundless journey, with magic to lend.

Through starlit corridors, we glimmer and glide,
Embracing the wonders that fates cannot hide.
In the heart of the night, let the dreams take wing,
For life is the music that dreams softly sing.

Gossamer Wings Across the Dawn

As dawn awakens with tender light,
Gossamer wings take to vibrant flight.
In the blush of morning, the world unfolds,
A symphony bright, in colors bold.

The sky is painted with whispers of gold,
Each ray a promise, a story untold.
With each gentle breeze, the day begins,
In the heart of the world, new magic spins.

Through fields of dreams, the light does dance,
A celebration of life, a joyful chance.
In every sunrise, the dreams will thrive,
Carried on wings, forever alive.

Harrowing Heights and Gentle Breezes

Upon the peaks where shadows dance,
A whisper flows, a fateful chance.
The winds, they sway like tales untold,
Of hearts entwined, of dreams so bold.

Through valleys deep, where secrets lie,
The echoes of old hopes still sigh.
With every step, the heavens call,
In gentle breezes, fears may fall.

The mountain's edge, the daring eyes,
Where laughter mingles with the skies.
With every breath, the world expands,
In solidarity, together we stand.

Yet shadows loom with creeping dread,
Of journeys past, of words unsaid.
But brave are those who seek the light,
For in the dark, they forge their flight.

So climb the heights, embrace the breeze,
For harrowing paths lead to ease.
In every heart, a flame ignites,
In harrowing heights, we find our sights.

Where Fantasies Take Flight

In moonlit realms where dreams arise,
The stars compose a vast disguise.
With every thought, a spark ignites,
In whispers soft, where magic writes.

As shadows stretch and day departs,
Imagination sings in hearts.
With wings of hope and beams of light,
We dance on air, our souls in flight.

On painted skies, our visions soar,
Beyond the clouds, we yearn for more.
Each fleeting moment conjures glee,
In realms where no one can foresee.

Through realms unknown, together we race,
In every corner, we find our place.
With fantasies that guide our way,
We'll chase the dawn, defy the gray.

So let us dream and let us climb,
In joyful leaps, we conquer time.
Where fantasies prevail, we ignite,
A tapestry woven, day or night.

The Allure of Celestial Heights

In twilight's glow, the stars align,
A dance of fate, a grand design.
With every wish upon the night,
We glimpse the path where dreams take flight.

Above the clouds, the heavens sing,
Of distant lands and what they bring.
The allure of heights, both bold and bright,
Calls forth the souls craving the light.

In starlit pools of cosmic grace,
We find our strength, we find our place.
The whispers of the universe,
Guide every traveler through each verse.

As galaxies spin and comets blaze,
We wander through a timeless maze.
In every heartbeat, the cosmos stirs,
The allurement of infinity blurs.

So take my hand, let us ascend,
Beyond the world, where wonders blend.
In celestial hearts, our spirits thrive,
In heights above, we feel alive.

Brushstrokes Across the Firmament

With colors bright, the skies entreat,
A canvas vast where dreams can meet.
Each brushstroke whispers tales of old,
Of daring hearts and journeys bold.

The sun dips low, a fiery blaze,
As shadows dance in evening's haze.
Each hue a note in twilight's song,
Where artists dwell and spirits throng.

Beneath the stars, we weave our dreams,
In galaxies of endless themes.
With every stroke, the memories gleam,
A tapestry of life's grand scheme.

Through cosmic realms, our stories blend,
An artful journey with no end.
In every corner, a spark ignites,
Brushstrokes across celestial heights.

So paint the night with all your heart,
Create a world, a vital part.
For in the sky, our hopes take flight,
Brushstrokes of life, pure and bright.

Fantasies Found Among the High Currents

In whispers soft where rivers glide,
Dreams take flight on currents wide,
Golden fish in sapphire streams,
Chase the shadows of our dreams.

Above the banks where willows weep,
Secrets murmur, ancient, deep,
Every ripple shows a tale,
Carried forth by wind and sail.

In twilight's glow, the stars align,
Magic weaves through pine and vine,
The air is thick with thoughts unspoken,
Promises made, though hearts be broken.

Through the mist where fairies dart,
Listen close to nature's heart,
Fantasies dance in twilight's haze,
Echoing through the secret bays.

The moon peeks through a silken cloud,
Casting light, both fierce and proud,
In these waters, dreams renew,
Fantasies thrive, forever true.

Illusions in the Dance of Skylines

Above the rooftops, shadows play,
As colors blend at close of day,
Each silhouette tells stories grand,
In the realm of the artist's hand.

Skyward leaps the daring kite,
In laughter shared, our spirits light,
Dreams hang high, like stars they gleam,
Illusions spun from wish and dream.

The city breathes, in ebb and flow,
Beneath the lights, the magic grows,
Waltz with fate as night descends,
Every heartbeat, a path that bends.

Whispers rise on every breeze,
Encouraged by the swaying trees,
In this dance, we come alive,
Holding fast, we learn to thrive.

Through every crevice, hope will shine,
In fragile dreams, our souls entwine,
The skyline swirls in hues so bright,
Illusions spark with gentle light.

The Guardians of Airborne Threads

Above the clouds where eagles soar,
Guardians watch from heaven's door,
Weaving tales on gossamer strands,
Touching hearts in distant lands.

A tapestry of stars unfolds,
Mysteries wrapped in whispers bold,
Each thread, a story, rich and rare,
In windswept dreams, we find our air.

With every gust, a secret flows,
As sunlight dances, softly glows,
Beneath their wings, the world awakes,
In every heart, the spirit breaks.

Among the heights where shadows drift,
The guardians lead, providing lift,
Airborne whispers of wishes shared,
In the web of fate, we are bared.

Together strong, these threads we weave,
In unity, we learn to believe,
Guard your dreams, let them take flight,
In the embrace of endless night.

Threads of Destiny Shining Alight

In twilight's glow, they bind and flow,
Threads of fate, through time they'll show,
On every path, in shadows bright,
Destiny whispers, 'Trust the light.'

Each moment stitched, with care and grace,
In every heart, we find our place,
With gentle hands, we shape and mold,
A tapestry of dreams retold.

Through storms and trials, we adhere,
The fabric woven, crystal clear,
With courage sewn into our seams,
We navigate our hopes and dreams.

In countless hues, the stories blend,
As lives entwine, they twist and bend,
Though time may fray the finest threads,
Resilience shines, and hope embeds.

So let us thread the needle true,
With every stitch, we start anew,
In destiny's grasp, we take our flight,
Threads of fate shine ever bright.

Wings of Tomorrow's Legends

In the hush of dawn's embrace,
Dreams take flight on whispered grace.
Feathers woven from hopes so bright,
They soar beyond the morning light.

Through valleys deep where shadows creep,
Courage calls and secrets keep.
With every heartbeat, tales unfold,
Of heroes brave and spirits bold.

In skies of azure, vast and wide,
A journey waits, with stars as guide.
The echoes of the past resound,
As future's whispers all around.

With wings adorned in colors rare,
They conquer fears, rise without care.
Each legend born, a spark ignites,
In hearts anew, through endless nights.

So spread your wings, let courage swell,
For tomorrow's legends, we shall tell.
In unity, let spirits fly,
Beneath the vast, unyielding sky.

The Dance of Light and Shadow

In this realm where twilight blends,
The dance begins, as daylight ends.
With every step, the silhouettes sway,
A tapestry spun from night and day.

With flickers bright and whispers low,
The balance holds, the shadows flow.
As moonbeams tease the dreams of night,
They beckon forth the softest light.

Twisting forms in twilight's trance,
A fleeting glimpse, a fleeting chance.
With every turn, the world stands still,
As time unwinds, it bends to will.

In harmony, the light will rise,
Embracing dark with tender sighs.
With every pulse, the story grows,
A secret dance that never slows.

So linger here, where magic glows,
In the space where balance flows.
Embrace the dance, let spirits soar,
For light and shadow, forevermore.

Veils of the Imagination Untethered

Beyond the edges of the known,
Imagination's seeds are sown.
In whispered dreams, a spark ignites,
Unraveling veils of endless nights.

With every vision, colors dance,
In realms where thoughts and wishes prance.
A canvas vast, awaiting strokes,
Where tales are spun and laughter pokes.

In fleeting glimpses, shadows play,
As thoughts run wild and drift away.
A journey forged in quiet grace,
In the mind's mirror, find your place.

So dare to dream, let visions fly,
Through whispered winds, across the sky.
For worlds unseen await your gaze,
In the magic of imagination's maze.

With every heartbeat, soar and dive,
In boundless realms, we come alive.
Embrace the magic, let it be,
The veils untamed, forever free.

Voices Lost Among the Stars

In the tapestry of the night,
Whispers drift like stars in flight.
From cosmic realms, where dreams converge,
Echoes rise, the silence purge.

Each twinkling light, a tale unfolds,
Of secrets kept and legends told.
Through galaxies of hope and fear,
Voices whisper for those who hear.

Beneath the moon's ethereal glow,
The lost find solace, hearts will know.
In distant realms, their songs reside,
A cosmic dance, where sorrow hides.

In astral sea, the memories gleam,
Of love and loss, a shared dream.
Through endless skies, their spirits roam,
Among the stars, they find a home.

So listen close to what they say,
For in the dark, they lead the way.
In voices lost, we find our part,
As starlight paints upon the heart.

Enigma of the Heavenly Wires

In the night, a whisper grows,
Threads of light like silver prose.
Dancing stars weave tales untold,
Secrets of the skies unfold.

A tapestry of cosmic dreams,
Where destiny and fate it seems,
Are tied with care in celestial knots,
An enigma that time forgot.

Through shadows deep where starlight glows,
A path emerges, ever flows.
With hope we tread on trails of beams,
In search of truth, or so it seems.

Each flicker holds a story bright,
Of ancient realms and endless night.
The wires hum a timeless song,
A melody where we belong.

To follow where the skylines blend,
Our hearts, our minds, in quest to mend.
In every spark, a dream ignites,
An enigma of the heavenly lights.

The Quest for Luminescent Pathways

Beneath the moon's soft, silver glow,
A journey starts, we're bound to go.
Through mystic woods and shining streams,
We seek the light that softly beams.

With every step, the shadows dance,
An invitation to take a chance.
Glowing pathways call us near,
In twilight's hush, we lose all fear.

Wisps of magic in the air,
Guiding us to treasures rare.
Luminescent trails, aglow,
Reveal the wonders we can't know.

The stars align, our hearts unite,
In search of dawn, away from night.
As every pathway shines anew,
Our quest reveals what once was true.

With courage found in fleeting light,
We chase the dreams that take to flight.
In every glow, a whisper speaks,
A quest fulfilled, as destiny seeks.

Celestial Bridges Under Twilight

As daylight fades to hues of gold,
Celestial bridges, tales unfold.
Arching high through skies so vast,
Connecting futures, present and past.

Under twilight's gentle embrace,
Dreams are woven, finding space.
The stars align, a serene guide,
On these bridges, we abide.

With hope, we leap from star to star,
Bound by wonders near and far.
Held by light, a sacred trust,
In starlit paths, we rise from dust.

Each step we take, the universe sighs,
Beneath the watch of countless eyes.
Together, we will forge a way,
On heavenly bridges where dreams sway.

With whispered winds that softly call,
We find our place, we won't let fall.
In every gasp of twilight's glow,
Celestial bridges lead us so.

Stories Cast in Featherlight Hues

In whispers soft, the breezes tell,
Stories cast like shimmering swell.
Featherlight hues in the twilight air,
A dance of dreams, beyond compare.

Where shadows play and colors blend,
Our imaginations will transcend.
Each feather floats on gentle flight,
A tale of longing, love, and light.

The moonlight weaves, a silver thread,
Through every dreamer's thoughts unsaid.
With every flicker, life renews,
In stories spun from featherlight hues.

Embrace the magic in the night,
Find joy in every whispered light.
For in these tales, our hearts take wing,
In feathered words, the world will sing.

So close your eyes, let visions flow,
In featherlight hues, the dreams will grow.
Stories cast in twilight's breath,
Are whispers of love that conquer death.

Cloudbound Echoes of Adventure

Above the world where dreams take flight,
Whispers dance in the soft twilight.
Clouds like ships on oceans vast,
Charting tales of the glorious past.

With every breeze, a story spins,
Of heroic deeds, where the laughter grins.
Across the skies, the echoes roam,
In every heart, we find our home.

The sun dips low, casting gold,
Secrets unfurl in colors bold.
Adventures beckon from every hive,
In the realm of dreams, we feel alive.

In every swirl, a journey wakes,
Through starlit paths, our spirit breaks.
With wings unbound, we soar and dive,
In the echoing clouds, our hopes survive.

The Weavers of Wind and Wonder

In twilight's hush, where shadows weave,
The weavers craft what none believe.
Threads of gold and silver light,
Spin tales that shimmer in the night.

With gentle hands, they stitch the air,
Creating dreams free from despair.
Every gust a tale to tell,
In the heart of dawn, where magic dwells.

Swaying branches, whispers soft,
In nature's cradle, we drift aloft.
Wonders bloom in every sigh,
In the hands of the weavers, we learn to fly.

Through every storm, a tapestry bright,
Embraced by hope, born of the night.
The symphony of stars above,
Guides our hearts to seek and love.

Enigmas of the Celestial Tapestry

Stars reveal their ancient lore,
In the vastness, we seek for more.
Patterns dance in cosmic light,
Whispers of secrets, dark and bright.

Nebulas bloom, like dreams in flight,
Painting the heavens with pure delight.
Enigmas swirl in midnight's embrace,
In every twinkle, a hidden trace.

Galaxies spin, a wondrous guise,
Reflecting hope in weary eyes.
Stories woven in starlit seams,
Carry the weight of our lost dreams.

Through the dark, we chase the spark,
In the silence, we leave our mark.
The universe speaks in silent awe,
As we embrace its cosmic law.

Flight Patterns of Lost Legends

In the dusk where shadows play,
Legends whisper, fading away.
Wings of time brush across the night,
Carrying tales of forgotten flight.

Echoes linger in the moon's soft glow,
Stories forgotten, yet still flow.
Patterns drawn in the velvet sky,
In every sigh, the spirits fly.

Over mountains, through the trees,
Legends travel on the breeze.
Carving paths of olden grace,
In the heart of memory's embrace.

Each feathered flight a whispered prayer,
Tales entwined with fragrant air.
In dreams, we find their lost refrain,
Reviving legends once again.

Timeless Murmurs in the Upper Realms

In twilight's hush, the stars do gleam,
Whispers of ages, a celestial dream.
Beyond the clouds, where secrets flow,
Echoes of past in soft winds blow.

Through shadows cast by the moon's pale light,
Phantoms of knowledge take wondrous flight.
They sing of tales long lost to time,
In melodies sweet, so soft, so sublime.

Each flicker bright tells stories anew,
Of realms unseen, where dreams come true.
A gentle nudge from the cosmic sea,
Assuring that magic will always be.

So linger awhile in that silken air,
Let whispers weave wonders, beyond compare.
For in these realms where silence stirs,
We find the timeless, in murmurs' purrs.

Awaken the heart to the universe wide,
And dance with the stars, let spirits abide.
For timeless whispers are ever near,
In the upper realms, forever clear.

Halos of Memory in the Stratosphere

Among the clouds, where thoughts collide,
Halos of memory do softly glide.
With every breath, recollections bloom,
In the heart's embrace, dispelling gloom.

A tapestry spun by the hands of time,
Each thread a story, a rhythm, a rhyme.
In the softest glow, past joys entwine,
As laughter lingers, bright and divine.

Drifting like feathers on gentle streams,
These halos of memory cradle our dreams.
From high above, they weave their song,
An orchestra where the lost belong.

The stratosphere glows with a warm embrace,
As memories dance in a timeless space.
They shimmer like stars, in the night so clear,
Guiding our hearts through the shadows of fear.

So walk with the past, let it softly show,
The beauty of moments that ebb and flow.
For in every halo, we find our way,
To cherish the light of each golden day.

Whims of the Wandering Spirits

In the twilight haze, spirits frolic and play,
Whims of the wild in a mystical ballet.
They swirl like leaves in a gentle breeze,
Whispering secrets among ancient trees.

With laughter that melts in the cool night air,
They dance upon shadows, without a care.
Each flicker of light is a heartbeat's grace,
As time holds its breath in this enchanted space.

Their playful essence, a shimmer of joy,
Brings life to the still, like a precious toy.
They twine and weave through the fabric of dreams,
A tapestry rich with glimmering beams.

So heed their call, let your spirit soar,
Embrace the unknown, yearn for more.
For whims of the spirits are yours to keep,
In the realms of wonder, where shadows leap.

In the still of the night, their tales unfold,
A saga of wonder, enchanting and bold.
With hearts intertwined, let the journey begin,
For the whims of the wandering spirits beckon us in.

Beyond the Reach of Earthly Eyes

In a world unseen, where shadows entwine,
Lie secrets so deep, like aged, fragrant wine.
Beyond the reach of the earthly sight,
Lies a realm that dances in ethereal light.

With whispers of time in the softest night,
The veils grow thin, unveiling pure light.
In realms where the fleeting gives rise to the true,
Yearnings awaken, forever anew.

Every glimmer calls to the heart from afar,
Drawing us closer like a radiant star.
In the silence of moments, we touch the sublime,
Where love outlasts even the march of time.

So gaze to the heavens with wide-open eyes,
And seek the marvels that never say die.
For in every glint of the mysteries wide,
Lies magic and wonder, in which we abide.

Beyond earthly realms, where the spirit flies free,
Unchained by the bonds of our mortal decree.
So soar into dreams, where the heart truly lies,
And discover the treasures that bloom in the skies.

Enchantments from the Whispering Skies

In twilight's glow, secrets alight,
The stars awaken, casting their might.
Whispers of magic swirl in the air,
As dreams take flight on a song of despair.

Beneath the vast and endless expanse,
Moonbeams beckon, inviting a dance.
The night blooms softly, a tapestry spun,
Where wishes converge, and lost hopes are won.

With each gentle breeze, stories emerge,
Unraveled by starlight, they silently surge.
Their echoes resound in the depths of the heart,
Enchantments that weave, never to part.

In the arms of the night, let courage unfold,
A wondrous adventure, like legends of old.
As shadows entwine, the magic ignites,
Where dreams and reality mingle in flight.

A symphony sung from the heavens above,
Awakens a longing, unshakeable love.
In each whispered note, a promise bestowed,
Enchantments shall linger, wherever we go.

Currents of Hope Spun Above

On the wings of dawn, new dreams arise,
As sunbeams scatter through azure skies.
Currents of hope, like rivers of light,
Guide weary souls toward what feels right.

With every heartbeat, a rhythm resounds,
In the silence of moments, clarity found.
Threads of connection stitch hearts as one,
Together we soar, reborn with the sun.

The skies painted gold, a canvas divine,
Promises linger where fate intertwines.
In shadows of doubt, our spirits ignite,
Currents of hope, leading us to the light.

Each challenge we face, a lesson in grace,
With laughter and tears, we grow in this space.
The tapestry woven, both fragile and bold,
Currents of hope, forever retold.

As stars fade away, and the daylight breaks,
We embrace the journey, whatever it takes.
With trust in the winds, we learn to believe,
Currents of hope, in which we conceive.

Ethereal Trysts with the Unknown

In the hush of twilight, secrets unwind,
Ethereal whispers, softly enshrined.
Trysts with the unknown, in shadows we dwell,
Where mysteries linger, enchantments compel.

Through the veil of night, the stars gently gleam,
Each flicker a glimpse of our wildest dream.
Paths intertwine in a dance of the brave,
Ethereal journeys through realms we crave.

A symphony beckons from beyond our sight,
In the depths of silence, we seek the light.
With hearts wide open, we venture, we roam,
Ethereal trysts, we find our way home.

With courage as armor and wonder as guide,
We traverse the borders where shadows abide.
In whispers of fate, the stories unfold,
Ethereal trysts with the unknown, retold.

In every heartbeat, in every sigh,
Magic awaits in the blink of the eye.
We grasp at the threads of a cosmic embrace,
Ethereal moments, a timeless grace.

Chronicles of the Feathered Heart

In forests deep, where the wild things play,
Chronicles whisper of night and of day.
Feathered hearts flutter, with stories to share,
Of journeys untraveled, of dreams laid bare.

With wings of the dawn, they lift off the ground,
In circles eternal, their freedom is found.
Each beat of their chests, a rhythm profound,
Chronicles echo where love knows no bounds.

Through storms they will rise, with tenacity bright,
Guided by moonbeams that pierce through the night.
In the tapestry woven, their colors ignite,
Chronicles of hope taking purposeful flight.

When shadows emerge, and doubt finds its way,
The feathered hearts gather, for light is their sway.
With strength in their song, they lift spirits high,
Chronicles sing through the vast, endless sky.

In every soft flutter, a promise remains,
For love is the thread that forever sustains.
In the heart's quiet chambers, their stories impart,
Chronicles treasured—the tales of the heart.

Celestial Ropes of Enchanted Skies

In twilight's glow, the stars do sew,
Celestial ropes that weave the show.
Each thread a tale, of night's embrace,
In whispered dreams, we find our place.

The moonlight dances on silver seas,
A symphony sung by ancient trees.
Through shadows deep, the spirits sway,
In harmony, they chase the day.

Chasing comets with grace untold,
They weave their dreams in threads of gold.
A flickering light, a shining spark,
Guides the way through the endless dark.

With every star, a wish is cast,
In the tapestry of night amassed.
Our hearts entwined, we gaze above,
In celestial wonders, we find love.

So hold the ropes that light the sky,
Let whispers echo, and spirits fly.
For in this realm of dreams so vast,
The magic binds, forever lasts.

Whispers of the Wind's Embrace

The wind does whisper, soft and light,
Through rustling leaves in gentle flight.
It carries tales from far away,
Of secrets sung at break of day.

In valleys deep, where shadows play,
The echoes of the past delay.
With every breeze, a memory,
Of ancient lands and skies set free.

Across the hills, the breezes chase,
A twirling dance, a sweet embrace.
With every gust, our worries fade,
In nature's song, we're unafraid.

The world awakens, soft and true,
As whispers come, a gentle cue.
Embrace the wind, let spirits soar,
For in its arms, we'll dream once more.

So listen close, with heart unbound,
For magic lies where winds are found.
In every sigh and laugh that plays,
The whispers guide us through the maze.

Unraveling the Secrets of Feathered Titans

High above where eagles soar,
The feathered titans guard their lore.
With wings outspread, they rule the sky,
In graceful arcs, they glide on high.

Through stormy clouds and sunlit beams,
They carry whispers, hopes, and dreams.
Each flap a story, each call a song,
In nature's choir, they belong.

From lofty heights, they see the earth,
A realm of beauty, love, and mirth.
Unraveling secrets held in flight,
Illuminated by a golden light.

In twilight's hush, their shadows fall,
As nightingale sings the dusk's sweet call.
With every beat, they show the way,
To hidden truths at end of day.

So let us dream of soaring high,
With feathered titans in the sky.
For in their flight, we find our peace,
In nature's arms, our worries cease.

Dreams Dangled from Ether's Edge

In realms of dreams where starlight gleams,
We dangle hopes from ether's seams.
With every breath, a wish takes flight,
In slumber's arms, we grasp the night.

Like lanterns swaying in the breeze,
Our visions dance among the trees.
With every flicker, a story told,
Of love and wonder, bright and bold.

Through gilded gates where shadows play,
The dreams illuminate the way.
With every heartbeat, joy unfolds,
In shimmering hues of silver gold.

As dawn approaches, dreams take flight,
Into the arms of morning light.
For every dream that we hold dear,
Is a promise whispered, always near.

So let us weave these visions bright,
On ether's edge, in realms of light.
For in our hearts, the dreams will stay,
To guide our steps through night and day.

Legends Carried by the Breeze

In ancient woods where shadows play,
The stories whisper, old and gray.
With every sigh, the branches sway,
As legends rise and drift away.

The echoes dance in twilight's glow,
Of heroes past, they come and go.
Their heartbeats thrum, a soft tableau,
In leaves that shimmer, tales bestow.

A breeze of time, a gentle guide,
Through realms where dreams and spirits bide.
With whispers bold, they're amplified,
In every heart, they gently slide.

The moonbeam's gaze, a silver thread,
Weaves through the words that once were said.
Together bound, the dreamers led,
By stories sung of those long dead.

So listen close, with open eyes,
To whispered truths beneath the skies.
In every rustle, life defies,
For legends carried, never die.

The Grand Tapestry of Flight

Above the world, where dreams take wing,
The skies weave tales of hope and spring.
Through clouds of gold, the sparrows sing,
In harmony, hearts begin to cling.

Each feathered dance a story spun,
In sunlit rays, the journeys run.
From dawn's first light, till day is done,
The canvas glows, the race is won.

On whispered winds, the echoes soar,
Of wanderers who seek for more.
They chase the stars, the ocean's roar,
A tapestry with threads galore.

Through Gentle breezes, dreams entwine,
In spirals soft, they intertwine.
With every heart a sacred sign,
That flight is free and wholly divine.

So let your spirit rise and glide,
Embrace the winds, the endless tide.
In every journey, love's the guide,
In the grand tapestry, we confide.

Celestial Voyagers in The Night

Amidst the stars, so far, yet near,
The cosmos hums, a tune to hear.
Each flicker bright, a tale, my dear,
Of voyagers lost, or ones held dear.

The velvet sky, a stage of dreams,
Where stardust flows in silvery streams.
With whispered wishes, bright beams gleam,
Celestial dance, some grander schemes.

Through constellations, paths unfold,
With every journey, stories told.
Their secrets kept, in nights so bold,
In twinkling stars, our fates enfold.

When twilight falls, and shadows creep,
The universe conspires deep.
In every heart, its mysteries seep,
As wanderers dream, and night winds weep.

So gaze above, let spirits rise,
For in the dark, the magic lies.
With open hearts to seek the skies,
The cosmos calls, through endless ties.

The Whispering Winds of Tomorrow

In dawn's embrace, the whispers call,
Through glades of green and shadows tall.
The winds of change, they gently sprawl,
Guiding us forth, to rise or fall.

With every breeze, a promise flows,
Of paths ahead, where bright hope glows.
In whispered tones, the future shows,
A world reborn, where love bestows.

The rustling leaves, they seem to share,
The dreams we sow, with tender care.
In every gust, a silent prayer,
To shape the dawn, a future rare.

The winds will guide our bounded souls,
Through unmarked trails, where courage rolls.
With hearts ablaze, the passion goals,
Together forging, our shared controls.

So heed the winds, let go of fears,
For in their breath, the magic steers.
To tomorrow's hope, and joyful tears,
With whispered winds, the future nears.

The Gathering of Celestial Echoes

In twilight's embrace, whispers sigh,
Stars weave tales in the velvet sky.
Moonlight dances on waves of blue,
Each heartbeat hums, a secret true.

Like shadows cast by ancient trees,
We drift along the evening breeze.
Echoes of laughter fill the air,
Memories linger, spun with care.

In the gathering dusk, glimmers spark,
A tapestry bright against the dark.
With every twinkle, hopes take flight,
Guided by dreams in the soft night.

As constellations begin to gleam,
We find our way through the midnight dream.
A celestial dance of fate and chance,
In the silence, our spirits prance.

So let us gather, hearts entwined,
In every echo, love defined.
Together we'll weave a cosmic song,
In the gathering of echoes, we belong.

Mirage of Enchanted Heights

Upon the cliffs where fairies dwell,
A mirage speaks, casting its spell.
Whispers linger in the golden light,
Calling forth dreams to take their flight.

With each step on this mystic path,
We chase the echoes of nature's wrath.
The air is thick with wonder's bloom,
As enchantment glides, banishing gloom.

The heights reveal a world untold,
Where secrets live and legends fold.
In twilight's glow, we seek and learn,
The lessons of the winds that churn.

Mirrors dance on the surface fair,
Reflecting hopes we'd long to share.
With every glance, we soar and dive,
In the mirage, our hearts revive.

So let us leap into the air,
Embrace the magic, shed our care.
In the heights where the spirits sing,
Together we'll find the joy of spring.

Spirits Ascendant in Thought

In the quiet corners of the mind,
The spirits whisper, ever kind.
They call us forth to seek the light,
In shadows deep, they forge our flight.

Through every doubt, they intertwine,
Threads of wisdom, pure and fine.
In silence, they dance, they glide,
Guiding us on this wondrous ride.

With thoughts like feathers in the breeze,
They lift our hopes with gentle ease.
Each moment bound in sacred grace,
In their presence, we find our place.

As spirits soar and shadows wane,
We learn to cherish joy and pain.
With every beat, our hearts align,
In the tapestry of the divine.

So let us gather, thought in flight,
Embracing dreams that shimmer bright.
With spirits ascendant, hearts expand,
In this realm where souls withstand.

Kaleidoscope of Dreams in Flight

Within the canvas of twilight's hue,
A kaleidoscope reveals the new.
Colors swirl in a playful dance,
Inviting us to take our chance.

Through shattered light, our visions bloom,
Casting away the weight of gloom.
Each shard reflects a universe wide,
Where hopes ignite and fears subside.

In dreams alight on the wings of night,
We chase the dawn, we seek the light.
With every flutter, shadows flee,
In this tapestry, we are free.

The essence of wonder fills the air,
Carried aloft on a winged prayer.
In the kaleidoscope's sweet embrace,
We find our truth, we find our place.

So let us revel in the delight,
Of dreams reborn in the gentlest light.
With hearts ablaze, we take to flight,
In the kaleidoscope of dreams so bright.

Fluttering Tales of Yore

In the forest where whispers dwell,
Ancient creatures weave their spell.
Leaves flutter softly, secrets untold,
Echoes of stories, in silver and gold.

Beneath the moonlight's tender gaze,
Stars twinkle brightly, guiding the ways.
Heroes and shadows dance and entwine,
In the heart of the woods, where dreams align.

With wings made of courage, they soar so high,
Over valleys and hills where the lost dreams lie.
Time drifts like feathers, a gentle embrace,
Each tale a treasure in a luminous place.

The winds carry laughter, and sometimes a sigh,
When stories like fireflies begin to fly.
Fables from ages, both tender and bold,
Fluttering quietly, forever retold.

Pilgrims Amongst the Stars

On starlit paths, where wonders collide,
Travelers wander, with dreams as their guide.
Planets like lanterns, glowing so bright,
Calling the seekers to dance in the night.

Constellations whisper of journeys begun,
Navigating shadows, embracing the sun.
Each comet a promise, streaking the skies,
Tales of adventure in the wide-open eyes.

With hearts full of courage, they chart the unknown,
Amongst the vast cosmos, they've bravely grown.
Voices of starlight harmonize sweet,
In the chorus of worlds where the dreamers meet.

Through nebulae swirling in colors divine,
Pilgrims are wandering, forever they'll shine.
Casting their wishes like shells on the shore,
Finding their purpose in the cosmic lore.

Echoes in the Ether

In the stillness, where spirits play,
Echoes resound, guiding the way.
A tapestry woven of sighs and laughs,
Threads of existence, in delicate drafts.

The air is alive with stories unspoken,
Words like soft feathers, gently woven.
Whispers of wisdom, from ages past,
Filling the silence, a spell to cast.

In the corners of night, where shadows creep,
Echoes awaken, secrets to keep.
Like ripples in water, they twist and they roam,
Bringing the wanderers softly back home.

Through the ether they linger, both fragile and bright,
Imprints of moments, lost in the light.
Each note a reminder that forever we'll be,
Bound by the echoes of eternity.

Lattices of Light and Shadow

In the lattice of dreams where shadows reside,
Light weaves through darkness, a seamless tide.
Figures take shape, both tender and frail,
Caught in the midst of a delicate veil.

A dance of reflections, the heart starts to race,
Finding the balance in an ethereal space.
Each flicker of hope, a beacon to guide,
Through the labyrinth pathways where spirits confide.

With every heartbeat, the patterns unfold,
Stories of courage, both timid and bold.
In the play of the shadows, a truth will emerge,
Bringing forth visions where destinies surge.

A symphony crafted from silence and sound,
In the lattices woven, true wonders abound.
For light and for shadow, forever entwined,
A tapestry vibrant, where dreams are designed.

The Weavers of Celestial Dreams

In twilight's glow, their handiwork shines,
Threads of silver, moonlit designs.
With whispers soft, they hum a tune,
Crafting dreams beneath the moon.

Each stitch a wish, each fold a lore,
They weave the night, a cosmic store.
With starlit fingers, I watch in awe,
As they shape the night, silent and raw.

Their loom spins magic, ethereal flight,
In the darkened skies, they dance with light.
A tapestry bright, where wishes entwine,
In the fabric of dreams, where hearts align.

Through galaxies vast, they gently reach,
In rippling patterns, they softly teach.
Of hope and love, of fears set free,
In the web of night, they beckon me.

So when the stars in their glory gleam,
Remember the weavers of our dreams.
With every twinkle, let your heart soar,
For they stitch the night with forevermore.

Navigating Through the Canvas of Air

With wings of gossamer, they glide afar,
Dancing on whispers, beneath each star.
Navigating dreams on a canvas blue,
They sketch the paths that the winds pursue.

In harmony, they trace the skies,
With laughter spun from the clouds' soft sighs.
Each movement a brushstroke in perfect grace,
Painting the heavens, a boundless space.

Through currents swift, they weave and dive,
On threads of air, they come alive.
With every spiral, a story unfurls,
Echoing softly, the heart of the world.

They gather the dreams that the night does weave,
In cushions of silk, we dare to believe.
As echoes of laughter drift through the night,
They sketch out our hopes, shining so bright.

So let us take flight, beneath the great dome,
For in the sweet air, we are never alone.
We'll dance with the breezes, a joyous affair,
Navigating through the vast canvas of air.

Echoes of Legends in the Stratosphere

In the pristine heights where legends soar,
Resonant whispers from ages before.
The stratosphere hums with stories untold,
Of heroes and myths, of brave and bold.

On wings of wonder, their echoes resound,
In the shimmering heights where dreams are found.
Each note a memory, each chord a plea,
Binding our past to the world we see.

Through the veils of time, their voices entwine,
Where stardust sparkles, their fates align.
With every heartbeat, a tale takes flight,
Painting the cosmos with luminous light.

In skies alive with the past's embrace,
We feel their journeys, we glimpse their grace.
Carried by winds, they guide us anew,
As echoes of legends, they call to you.

So let us honor these spirits on high,
With hearts wide open, we aim for the sky.
For in every echo, in every cheer,
Lies the magic of legends, forever near.

Between the Stars, a Tapestry of Man

Between the stars, our stories reside,
A tapestry woven, in starlight we glide.
Threads of our joy, strands of our pain,
Together they shimmer, in wild refrain.

Through trials and triumphs, each life a thread,
In the grand design, we wander and tread.
With hearts of courage, we dream and we dare,
For woven together, we rise through despair.

In every heartbeats' echo, we find our place,
Intertwined destinies in the celestial space.
From the ashes of sorrow, the brilliance will glow,
Tapestry binding us through every flow.

On pathways of stardust, we dance through the night,
Each step a promise, a flicker of light.
Between the stars, we are never alone,
For in this vast canvas, our spirits have grown.

So let us embrace the threads that we share,
The laughter, the love, and moments most rare.
For between the stars, in the cosmic span,
We are threads of a story, a tapestry of man.

Fables Scattered on the Winds

Whispers dance upon the breeze,
Tales of yesteryears and dreams.
Each story spun with gentle ease,
A tapestry of thought it seems.

Amongst the leaves the secrets hide,
In shadows where the lost ones sigh.
The fables tell of heart and pride,
As starlit nights drift gently by.

With every gust, a memory stirred,
Of laughter, love, and tears once shed.
The softest truth is always heard,
In winds that carry words unsaid.

A sailor's song on ocean's crest,
A lullaby of storms once faced.
With each horizon's fervent quest,
Hearts bound by dreams shall not be chased.

So listen close, in silence glean,
The stories scattered on the air.
For in those fables, life is seen,
A wisdom woven everywhere.

Latticework of Dreams Above

Starlit threads between our wishes,
Weave a fabric, fine and bright.
In each glimmer, hope replenishes,
A gentle guide through darkest night.

Beneath the vast, celestial dome,
Our thoughts entwine like silver strings.
In this expanse, we find our home,
A cradle where the moonlight sings.

Each twinkling star, a promise made,
That dreams can soar and find their flight.
With every heartbeat, fears do fade,
As we embrace the endless night.

Let whispers rise on whispered winds,
From depths of heart to heights above.
For in this space where magic spins,
We craft our world with thread of love.

So gaze upwards, let spirit soar,
At latticework of dreams aglow.
For in the sky, forevermore,
The spark of hope shall ever flow.

Glimpses Beyond the Twilight Veil

In twilight's hush, a soft refrain,
Flickers dance in dusky light.
A world unseen, where dreams remain,
In shadows cast by fading bright.

Around the edges of the day,
Echoes call from realms afar.
We glimpse the magic, hear its play,
In whispers soft, like ancient stars.

Each sighing breeze brings tales untold,
Of spirits waiting, ever near.
In twilight's grasp, the brave and bold,
Shall see the paths that weave from fear.

So take a step through veil so thin,
Where wonders wait for hearts to feel.
Beyond the dusk, where dreams begin,
The twilight's magic, pure and real.

In every heartbeat, life anew,
A dance of shadows starts to sway.
In glimpses found, a truth so true,
Beyond the twilight's slow decay.

An Odyssey of Wings and Spirits

On feathers soft, the spirits glide,
Across the skies, in endless roam.
With every beat, their hearts abide,
In quests for warmth, they call it home.

Through valleys deep and mountains high,
They chase the dawn with pure delight.
In every whisper of the sky,
An odyssey unfolds in flight.

With laughter bright as morning rays,
They weave through dreams like silver beams.
In sacred woods where shadows play,
Their voices echo woven schemes.

On winds that carry tales of old,
Their journeys dance like autumn leaves.
In every spirit brave and bold,
A tapestry of life believes.

So as the night gives way to dawn,
And shadows melt with coming light,
Remember those who softly yawn,
In odyssey of wings and flight.

For in their glide, our hopes shall soar,
An endless blessing, ever near.
Together in this world, we're more,
As wings and spirits intertwine here.

The Call of the Ethereal Traveler

In an echoing silence, I hear a song,
Whispers of places where spirits belong.
With starlit paths woven deep in the night,
I follow the call of the ethereal light.

Through valleys of shadow and mountains of mist,
The traveler beckons, I cannot resist.
Each step is a thread in a mystical scheme,
A tapestry woven from hope and a dream.

From forests enchanted where moonbeams do dance,
To shores of the ocean, an infinite expanse.
The stars are my compass, the wind in my sail,
Guiding my journey where destinies prevail.

With each fleeting moment, new wonders unfold,
Tales of the lost, in the night they are told.
Time bends like the rivers, no end to explore,
As I chase the horizon, forever and more.

In the heart of the twilight, a promise I see,
That beyond every shadow, I might find me free.
Thus, onward I wander, through realms unforeseen,
The call of the traveler, forever my dream.

Captivating Currents of the Wind

The wind sings a melody, soft and serene,
Carrying secrets of places unseen.
In sighs and in whispers, it beckons my soul,
To dance with the currents, to rise and to roll.

Each gust is a story, a tale from afar,
Of mountain peaks high and the wandering stars.
With wings made of wanderlust, I will take flight,
Guided by breezes that cut through the night.

From forests of emerald, to deserts of gold,
The wind calls my spirit, adventurous, bold.
It flows through the valleys, it sweeps o'er the plains,
In every soft rustle, its music remains.

As clouds turn to whispers, embracing the sky,
I dance on the edges where earth meets the high.
The stories it carries, through ages and time,
Are woven with magic, a rhythm, a rhyme.

So I follow the whispers, the breath of the air,
With grace of the willows and wild with flair.
For in every current, a promise lies free,
The captivating wind sings its song just for me.

Mythos of the Winged Wanderer

High above the valleys, where eagles reside,
The winged wanderer soars with pride.
With feathers of twilight and eyes full of fire,
He carries the dreams of those who aspire.

In the hush of the dawn, his call fills the air,
A spirit untamed, free from all care.
He dances with clouds, in a sky made of blue,
A myth born of legends, forever brand new.

Embracing the tempest, he rides the fierce storm,
A symbol of courage in every form.
His flight weaves a tale upon zephyrs unseen,
Of worlds intertwined and desires serene.

And when shadows gather, he lights up the gloom,
With a heart made of starlight and an aura of bloom.
His journey reflects, the wonders we seek,
A reminder to all, life is lush, not bleak.

In the hush of the twilight, his silhouette glows,
A guardian of dreams that everyone knows.
For in the sky's canvas, he paints with the dawn,
The mythos of wanderers, forever reborn.

Threads of Fate in the Firmament

High in the cosmos, where destinies blend,
Threads of fate shimmer, a story to send.
In the fabric of starlight, our paths intertwine,
A dance of connection, a tapestry fine.

Each twinkle a moment, each glow a new chance,
To follow the rhythm, to leap and to dance.
The constellations guide us through shadows and light,
Weaving our futures in the depth of the night.

With whispers of starlings that flutter above,
These threads bound by hope, tender ties of love.
In the canvas of heavens, our fears are erased,
As we navigate time, through the vast and the chaste.

As comets streak by, they spark joy and dread,
In the grand design where our stories are bred.
Each thread holds a secret, a wish long desired,
In the realm of the cosmos, our spirit is fired.

So look to the heavens, let your heart take flight,
For each thread is a promise, a beacon of light.
In the firmament's embrace, our destinies play,
A symphony woven, come join in the sway.

The Flight of Mythical Looms

In twilight's soft embrace they glide,
With feathers kissed by starlit skies.
Each beat a call to worlds untried,
A fable woven through the lies.

From shadowed groves to moonlit streams,
Their whispers dance on evening air.
In dreams, they stir forgotten dreams,
A promise sparkles everywhere.

The world below, a canvas wide,
As myths entwine in every breeze.
They ride the winds, these silken guides,
Emboldened by the whispered pleas.

Through realms of wonder, bold and bright,
They paint the night with visions rare.
Each tale a thread of pure delight,
In here, enchantments fold and flare.

So spread your arms and take to flight,
With looms that spin the sky's own grace.
For in the heart of endless night,
Awaits the magic we must trace.

Threads Woven in Celestial Tapestries

In silken strands of lunar glow,
The weavers hum a tune of lore.
Through cosmic realms where breezes blow,
Their stories shimmer evermore.

With fingertips of stardust dreams,
They stitch the fabric of the skies.
Each stitch a part of destiny's seams,
Where time and space begin to rise.

Among the galaxies, they play,
With colors bold that shift and swirl.
They craft the night and guide the day,
A dance of light in endless whirls.

As constellations weave their song,
The universe begins to sway.
In harmony, both fierce and strong,
The threads unite in grand array.

So let your spirit drift and soar,
Through tapestries of cosmic hue.
For every stitch, a tale in store,
As dreams unfold, both bright and new.

Soaring Hopes on Gossamer Wings

On gossamer wings, they rise so high,
With hopes unfurling in the light.
Each flutter whispers 'never die',
Carried on whispers of delight.

Through fields of dreams and skies of gold,
They dance amidst the warmest streams.
In every heart, a courage bold,
To lift their wings on soaring beams.

The sunbeam trails leave paths to chase,
As laughter sparks in vibrant flight.
In every corner, joy finds place,
A symphony of purest light.

So chase the winds on fate's own course,
Let every heartbeat be your guide.
For in the freedom lies the source,
Where hope and dreams forever glide.

Embrace the skies with spirit free,
For every struggle has its spring.
On gossamer wings, we'll come to be,
A testament to all we sing.

Between Cloud and Canopy: A Journey

Beneath the clouds, the whispers flow,
In canopies where secrets hide.
A journey starts with tales to know,
Where dreams and magic coincide.

Through woven branches, shadows play,
With every step, a world unfolds.
A hidden path, a soft ballet,
As ancient stories dare be told.

The brook's soft murmur guides us near,
To realms where time forever bends.
Where laughter flows and hearts feel clear,
And every journey never ends.

The sky above, a painted dome,
With hues of dusk and dawn's embrace.
In nature's arms, we find our home,
In every leaf, a timeless grace.

So step from shadow into light,
Let wonder spark your heart anew.
For in this world of pure delight,
The journey starts with me and you.

Threads of Ether and Imagination

In twilight's glow, the whispers rise,
A tapestry spun, beneath starlit skies.
Each thread a dream, woven with care,
In the loom of time, magic lays bare.

The echoes of laughter, the shadows of lore,
In the garden of thought, we seek to explore.
With every heartbeat, the stories unfold,
In the realm of the mind, where the brave are bold.

Through portals of wonder, we journey afar,
With friends by our side, like a guiding star.
Hand in hand, through enchantment we glide,
In the threads of ether, our spirits abide.

From whispers of dawn to the dusk's soft sigh,
With courage in heart, we shall learn to fly.
The wonders of magic, so vivid, so bright,
In the fabric of dreams, we craft our own light.

And when shadows linger, and fears come to play,
We clutch to our visions, come what may.
For in the world of stories, we carve our own fate,
With threads of imagination, we can create.

The Griffin's Dance in the Clouds

Above the world, where the sky kisses earth,
The griffins soar, full of grace and mirth.
With wings outstretched, they embrace the breeze,
In a dance of freedom that puts hearts at ease.

With a roar that echoes through valleys below,
The guardians of magic put on a show.
They twist and they twirl, in a sunlit array,
Guiding lost souls on their mystical way.

In the midst of the storm, they find their own calm,
Their powerful presence like a gentle balm.
With feathers aglow, in hues bold and bright,
They paint the sky's canvas with sheer delight.

Through fog and through rain, they unearth the sun,
In the dance of the griffins, all sorrows undone.
Each flap of their wings is a promise, a dream,
In this world of wonder, boundless and supreme.

So take to the heights where the wild things play,
And join in their dance, let your spirit sway.
For the griffin's embrace is a tale set alight,
In the clouds and the whispers, where magic takes flight.

Upward Bound: Tales of the Bold

With hearts alight and spirits unchained,
We venture forth, where the wild is unclaimed.
The path is uncertain, but dreams lead the way,
Through valleys of doubt, where the brave choose to stay.

The legends we weave, in the ink of our scars,
Are tales of the bold, who reach for the stars.
With laughter and courage, we face every test,
In the quest for the truth, in pursuit of the best.

Though shadows may linger, and storms may arise,
Our fearless hearts shine, like the brightest of skies.
With faith intertwined, in bonds that we hold,
We journey together, our tales to unfold.

From mountains so high to the depths of the sea,
The call of adventure is a sweet melody.
In the whispers of night, or in dawn's gentle light,
We strive for our visions, with all of our might.

And when the path narrows and darkness creeps near,
We find strength in each other, through love, through
cheer.
For in every tale, in the trials we face,
Is the journey of life, and its infinite grace.

Beyond the Horizon's Embrace

When the sun dips low and the stars take their place,
We dream of the lands that lie beyond space.
With hearts full of wonder and eyes open wide,
We chase after visions where secrets reside.

Beyond the horizon, where the wild things roam,
We seek the adventures that beckon us home.
With whispers of lore that the ancients once knew,
In the tapestry of time, we'll weave something new.

Through valleys of gold, and mountains of night,
We dance in the shadows, we bask in the light.
With every heartbeat and every soft sigh,
We soar with the eagles, we learn how to fly.

In the realm of the dreamers, we find our own way,
Through storms and through calm, we embrace the ballet.

Together we journey, through laughter and tears,
In the whispers of time, we conquer our fears.

So let the horizons beckon, let the wild winds call,
For the journey is ours, and we'll never be small.
In the embrace of the dawn, we'll canvas the sky,
Beyond the horizon, we'll learn how to fly.

Soaring High on Dreams' Power

In twilight's glow, we spread our wings,
Chasing hopes as the nightingale sings.
With whispered dreams, we lift from the ground,
In clouds of joy, where magic is found.

Through stardust journeys and midnight flights,
We journey, tracing the moon's soft lights.
Above the world, our spirits entwine,
In heights unknown, where wonders align.

The winds of fate guide our hearts so free,
As we ride the breeze, just you and me.
With every heartbeat, we dare to climb,
To realms uncharted, beyond space and time.

Let our laughter echo in the skies,
For in every flutter, a new dream lies.
Soaring high, we rise through night's embrace,
Finding our fortune in this boundless space.

In dream's embrace, we dance and twirl,
As galaxies spin and the stardust swirls.
With fearless hearts, we embrace the flow,
Soaring high, together, we glow.

Stratospheric Serenade

Above the clouds, where silence breaks,
The sky unveils what the heart forsakes.
In whispers sweet, the heavens sing,
Of tales untold, on a silver wing.

With every note, a wish takes flight,
Illuminating the velvet night.
A melody born from the soul's deep core,
It calls us to dance, forevermore.

We chase the comets through cosmic streams,
Awash in the glow of our wildest dreams.
Each star a friend, each wish a spark,
Lighting our path through the endless dark.

Beneath the moon's soft, watchful gaze,
We weave our stories through time's endless maze.
As notes entwine with the breeze's sigh,
In this stratospheric serenade, we fly.

United in song, our spirits soar,
With every chorus, we yearn for more.
Through rhythms grand, we rise and blend,
In harmony sweet, on dreams we depend.

Boundless Visions in the Air

In twilight realms where visions gleam,
We sail on dreams, a wondrous stream.
With whispered hopes, we carve the sky,
In boundless flight, we dare to try.

The stars align with a gentle grace,
As we find solace in this vast space.
With the whispers of the night below,
We chase the secrets the heavens show.

Each gust of wind, a guiding hand,
To worlds where only dreamers stand.
In every heartbeat, our visions flow,
As we embrace the magic we know.

With every moment, our dreams conspire,
To weave a tapestry of brave desire.
Set free your heart to soar anew,
In boundless realms where magic is true.

Through echoes bright, our spirits fly,
In endless skies where the eagles cry.
Each moment cherished, each dream laid bare,
In boundless visions, we find our care.

The Skylark's Lament

In dawn's first light, a skylark sings,
A tale of sorrow on fragile wings.
With mournful notes that pierce the air,
It paints the skies with its soft despair.

Among the clouds, it weaves its song,
Of joy once cherished but now gone wrong.
In every trill, a memory clings,
A wistful echo of what life brings.

The winds of change, they sweep and sigh,
As dreams once bright begin to die.
Yet in the heart, a flicker remains,
A whispered hope amid the pains.

With each sweet note, the skylark weaves,
A story wrapped in autumn leaves.
Though shadows linger where bright light bled,
The song persists though joy has fled.

So let us cherish every strain,
For in soft laments, we find our gain.
In sorrow's grip, a lesson lies,
To soar again beneath open skies.

9 781805 634515